CW01648723

Sixties Spotting Days Around London & the Home Counties

Strathwood

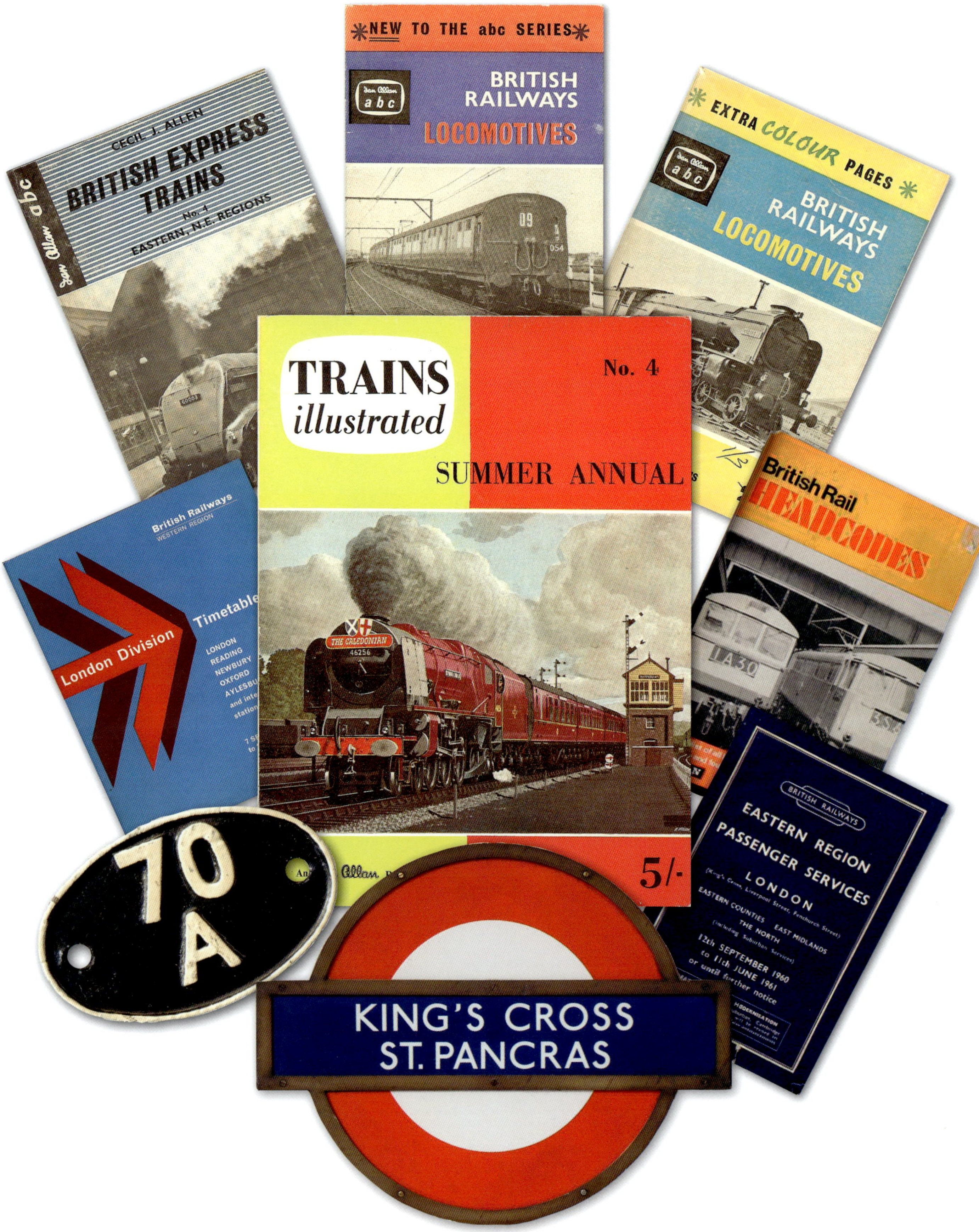
CECIL J. ALLEN
BRITISH EXPRESS TRAINS
No. 4
EASTERN, N.E. REGIONS
Ian Allan abc
NEW TO THE abc SERIES
Ian Allan abc
BRITISH RAILWAYS
LOCOMOTIVES
EXTRA COLOUR PAGES
Ian Allan abc
BRITISH RAILWAYS
LOCOMOTIVES
TRAINS illustrated
No. 4
SUMMER ANNUAL
THE CALEDONIAN
46256
5/-
British Railways
WESTERN REGION
Timetable
London Division
LONDON
READING
NEWBURY
OXFORD
British Rail
HEADCODES
BRITISH RAILWAYS
EASTERN REGION
PASSENGER SERVICES
LONDON
EASTERN COUNTIES EAST MIDLANDS
THE NORTH
12th SEPTEMBER 1960
to 11th JUNE 1961
or until further notice
70
A
KING'S CROSS
ST. PANCRAS

Sixties Spotting Days Around London & the Home Counties

Cover: The shunter leans back and admires 46155 The Lancer as they ready for departure from St.Pancras on 19 September 1964. The Royal Scot will take the special as far as Peterborough East and then run light to Nottingham Victoria to pick it up on the return run to Marylebone later in the day. ***Strathwood Library Collection***

Kevin Derrick

Strathwood

Sixties Spotting Days Around London & the Home Counties

First published 2013

ISBN 1-905276-33-8
ISBN 978-1-90276-33-2

All rights reserved. No part of this book may be reproduced or transmitted in any form or by any means, electronic or mechanical, including photocopying, recording or by any information storage and retrieval system, without written permission from the Publisher in writing.

Copyright Strathwood 2013

Published by Strathwood, 9 Boswell Crescent, Inverness, IV2 3ET Tel 01463 234004
www.strathwood.co.uk

Proudly printed in the United Kingdom

Contents

Page

Introduction 6

Euston to Watford 7

Back and Forth in Metroland 27

Follow the Thames 38

South Western Approach 60

Southern Surburbs 68

Majestic Midland 76

Kings Cross Modernisation 82

Great Eastern Rennaisance 88

Photographic Archive 96

Introduction

Above: The days for condensing apparatus fitted 3MT 40026 were now numbered by 7 June 1960 when it was recorded at Moorgate, withdrawl would take place in November two years later. ***Douglas Twibble***

Below: Two non-standard liveries peer out from the gloom that once was Liverpool Street station with Class J 69 68619 on station pilot duty in a reproduction of the Great Eastern Railway's colours and D5579 in an experimental Golden Ochre paint scheme on 6 February 1960. ***Douglas Twibble***

Travelling back in time to London as the 1960s dawned was to an era when even after fifteen years of peacetime the effects of the Blitz were still easy to see. It may seem like a lifetime ago, and it really was as your author recalls now well into his fifties who was just two at the start of the decade.

Having grown up in London during this period I was hopefully aware to what was happening around me, with some sadness I realise as so many do that my interests in life might have been better served if I had been born a few decades beforehand. A conversation with one older picture contributor who is now in his nineties revealed he too wished he had been born twenty years earlier so he could have seen and recalled the days of those extravagent liveries before the grouping of the railways in 1922! So I know I am not alone, hopefully this and other titles in the Sixties Spotting days series will bring enjoyment and happy memories to those who were there at the time and a realisation for those of us who were younger or perhaps born later, that we really did miss out on some interesting times.

My personal memories were based around Feltham in the early sixties and many days spent climbing on the rows of withdrawn steam engines, or perhaps waving to the drivers of the diesel shunters which had rendered these same steam locomotives surplus, for an unnofficial cab ride up and down the sidings within the once huge hump yards here.

With family connections in the north east I was over the moon at the prospect of a train ride from Kings Cross to Newcastle just after Christmas in 1962, and made a huge fuss to see the steam locomotive at the head of our train before I would agree to come quietly and get on the train at Kings Cross.

Then spotting on the long footbridge at Southall and the excitement of standing underneath a speeding train as it roared past covering one in its exhaust. Oh yes happy days, but tempered with memories of the desolation that quickly engulfed Feltham engine sheds and yards when steam vanished in 1967.

However I like many can associate some of these memories with the enjoyment of these colour photographs from the time, shared with us thanks to the kindness of our picture contributors. Maybe you took material in either colour or black and white from the period 1948 to 1979, if you did do get in touch and we can see some of it in print in future books perhaps.

Kevin Derrick
Inverness 2013

Euston to Watford

Platform end spotters are on hand to witness D5143 take out empty carriage stock made up from ex LMS vehicles on 3 June 1962 as a prelude of the great changes to come. ***Strathwood Library Collection***

Amid much public outcry, the old station building and the iconic Euston Arch were demolished in 1961-2 to be replaced by a new building. It's opening in 1968 followed the electrification of the West Coast Main Line, and the new structure was intended to symbolise the coming of the Electric Age, this view was taken just as the decade began. ***Frank Hornby***

For most of the mid-sixties passengers had to suffer the chaos of a major railway station being totally rebuilt, although much has been done to ensure the arrival of this Royal Train in 1964 behind 70021 Morning Star is as tidy as possible. ***Winston Cole***

By April 1967 the new image of British Rail was evident with E3181 and E3052 resplendent in their new Electric Blue liveries as they prepare to head north from London on the route of the former London & North Western Railway. ***Strathwood Library Collection***

Work for diesel locomotives similar to D5019 would remain for years to come in removing empty coaching stock to Stonebridge Park for servicing and storage as here on Camden Bank in September 1965. ***Dave Cobbe/Rail Photoprints***

Another shot taken on Sunday 3 June 1962 this time at Camden shed as 46200 The Princess Royal stands below the coaler, having recently arrived after hauling the last leg from Carlisle of the RCTS/SLS organised Aberdeen Flyer. The special had departed northwards the previous day from Kings Cross behind 60022 Mallard, and it was to have been the last steam-hauled Kings Cross to Edinburgh non-stop run with a crew change via the corridor tender. Sadly, in the event a preceding freight developed a hot box near Chathill, Northumberland, thus delaying the special and so the non-stop run was not achieved. ***Dave Cobbe/Rail Photoprints***

The crew look out from their comfortable cab as Standard 2MT 78063 makes its way light engine past Camden sheds in September 1963. The penultimate of her class of sixty five Darlington built locomotives, this example entered service in November 1956, just under seven years before this shot was taken, by the end of 1965 steam had vanished from ecs work out of Euston. ***Rail Photoprints***

Another crudely affixed headcode adorns 46246 City of Manchester in a more work weary condition to display it's maroon livery outside the running shed at Camden in June 1960 which the Stanier designs now have to share with English Electric Type 4 diesels. ***Ian Turnbull/Rail Photoprints***

Whilst Camden was coded 1B and often saw Stanier's Pacifics it closed to steam on 9 September 1963, it was Willesden coded 1A that outlasted for steam operations until 27 September 1965. Recently outshopped from Crewe Works was the un-named Patriot Class 45547 on 12 May 1961 among the ranks at Willesden. ***Strathwood Library Collection***

Whereas on 10 June 1964, Jinty 47501 was more typically covered in the effects of ash and everyday work as it stood in steam as the Willesden shed pilot. The previous month at nearby Wembley Stadium Bobby Moore had led West Ham United to victory 3-2 over Preston North End in that year's FA Cup Final. ***Peter Coton***

The fireman of 46240 City of Coventry makes haste alongside to deal with any points that need to be set as the Stanier Pacific's driver backs out from shed yard at Willesden on 18 August 1963. This fine locomotive would be withdrawn from service fourteen months later, whilst it was sadly scrapped one of the nameplates complete with the crest and and smokebox numberplate would later be affixed to the wall of the station concourse at Coventry station. ***Frank Hornby***

Another of Sir William Stanier's fine Pacifics 46230 Duchess of Buccleuch in a rather grubby green livery keeps company with some of the great CME's other designs at Willesden in July 1963. This example however was among those withdrawn during 1963, being taken out of service that November. ***Win Wall/Strathwood Library Collection***

A chance to compare two designs of British Railway's Standard Moguls at Willesden with firstly Class 4MT 76088 on 8 March 1964 which had been built at Horwich during 1957. ***Frank Hornby***

Whereas 78019 had entered service three years earlier after being built at Darlington to the 2MT design was also to be seen at on shed this time on 6 June 1965. ***Strathwood Library Collection***

Still looking smart although bereft of it's Anzac nameplates was Crewe built Class 7P6F Britannia 70046 among the outside stores at Willesden on 11 August 1963. ***Rail Photoprints***

Engaged in a little shed pilot work at Willesden on 25 March 1961 was North British built 42576 which was one of a large batch out-sourced by the LMS between 1935 and 1937 to Stanier's 2-Cylinder design of 2-6-4T. ***Strathwood Library Collection***

As a Londoner your author would have been very pleased if 46245 City of London had been chosen for preservation, but alas it was withdrawn in October 1964 and broken up within weeks! Just before this on 15 July that year an unknown cameraman has recorded this delightful view of the the locomotive in steam at Willesden. ***Strathwood Library Collection***

The first of the British Railway's built Britannia Pacifics, 70000 herself leads its much scruffier classmate 70050 Firth of Clyde off shed at Willesden in May 1964. Both locomotives had worked specials to Wembley that day, and both engines would be withdrawn during 1966, with Britannia avoiding the attentions of the scrap dealers fortunately becoming part of the National Collection. ***Bob Treacher/Alton Model Centre***

Another victim of the 1966 withdrawls would be Black Five 45434 which succumbed in September that year. We see the Armstrong Whitworth built locomotive making some smoke on shed at Willesden during 1962. ***Strathwood Library Collection***

Another of those train reporting number boards has been affixed to a truly filthy 70024 in the sunshine at Willesden on 21 September 1964, fortunately the Britannia Pacific still carries its Vulcan nameplates at this time. ***Dave Down***

We next make a move along the London District electrified suburban route alongside the West Coast Main Line to Wembley Central on 4 March 1961 to record firstly one of the LMS built EMUs which were soon to be replaced by British Railways built 3-Car sets later known as Class 501 units. The former LNWR and LMS units were replaced between 1960 and 1963 on the routes between Broad Steet and Richmond and from Euston to Watford Junction. In 1915 the Bakerloo Line was extended to Queen's Park, where it joined these DC electrified lines as far as Watford Junction. The London Transport Bakerloo Line services were operated with 1938 built stock and these services were to be reduced in this decade. ***Both: Frank Hornby***

The electrified route utilising four rails is seen alongside the West Coast Main Line at Kenton as 46234 Duchess of Abercorn speeds north adorned with The Caledonian headboard, this was a sevice linking Euston with Glasgow Central in August 1960, the coaches also carry suitable roof nameboards along their flanks. ***Robert Western***

The overhead wiring was in place as D380 made its way past Harrow & Wealdstone in 1964, where twelve years beforehand 112 people had been killed in the dreadfully disasterous rail smash here. ***Douglas Twibble***

Steam readily condenses in the cold air outside Watford shed 1C as Fairburn 2-6-4T 42096 stands in the sunshine in December 1962. ***Win Wall/Strathwood Library Collection***

A top up of water for Black Five, 45048 alongside Watford Junction station again on that same cold December morning in 1962, Watford shed would be closed to steam on 29 March 1965 and relegated to the status of a stabling point for diesels for a short while after this. ***Win Wall/Strathwood Library Collection***

A London Country RT bus is on a service crossing the bridge in the background as Royal Scot 46161 King's Own thunders past Watford's shed building and into the station with an up express on 4 March 1961. ***Frank Hornby***

Taken the same day was this view of Class 2P, 40657 as it too makes its way past the deserted Watford shed building. The 1931 Crewe built 4-4-0, would be taken out of traffic in October the following year. ***Frank Hornby***

We have already seen a view of 46200 The Princess Royal on page 10 taken on 3 June 1962, this was the scene at Watford Junction when a ten minute stop was scheduled during the Aberdeen Flyer Railtour at the station. The stop allowed the tour participants the chance to stretch their legs and grab a photograph, even though the train was running almost three hours late on it's timings for a two day railtour. ***Strathwood Library Collection***

The wires are up and the track is being renewed for full electrification at Watford Junction as our cameraman holds the gaze of the Station Master as Royal Scot 46152 The King's Dragoon Guardsman passes on the up line. **John Newman**

Back and Forth in Metroland

Watford enjoys five stations including this one exclusively served by London Transport's Metropolitan Line trains. By the time of this view on 4 March 1961, the 1927-31 built 'T' stock was already being replaced by the A60 and A62 stock, with the final 'T' stock train running on 5 October 1962. The 'Q' stock used for the District Line Centenary Tour on 24 August 1969 was also nearing the end of its reign too. ***Frank Hornby & Strathwood Library Collection***

The regular use of the ex-British Railway's Pannier Tanks on the trains to Watford Tip was a popular excuse for many enthusiasts to continue enjoying steam activity as main line use ceased in the Capital. On a sunny 30 April 1967, the empty return working is seen making its way through Northwood with L95 in charge. This example had joined the London Transport fleet in 1960, having been withdrawn from British Railways use as 5764, it went on to give active service until 1971, and enjoys life today in preservation as a result. ***John Green***

This was the first L91 which was 5752 which came to London Transport in 1956 it was withdrawn in 1960 and replaced with 5758 also allocated the same number L91, this one lasted until 1968. Also present at Neasden the same day was L48 which was one of seven locomotives built for the Metropolitan Railway in 1901. ***Both: Strathwood Library Collection***

To combat ice and snow build up on the conductor rails London Transport built a fleet of eighteen electric sleet locomotives from redundant motor cars from the former Central London Railway stock dating from 1903/4. This example ESL106, is seen at Neasden awaiting the return of the next bout of harsh weather. ***Aldo Delicata***

A visit inside the running shed at Neasden on 29 April 1967 finds among the ranks of Metropilitan Line A60 stock the venerable former Metropolitan Railway electric locomotive 1 John Lyon which was sadly scrapped in 1974. Behind is ESL107 which as the last of the electric sleet locomotives in service in 1985 was preserved by London Transport. ***Strathwood Library Collection***

Another of the Pannier Tanks to be replaced by a fresher example was L90, seen here at Neasden this is the first locomotive arriving as 7711 in 1956, to be replaced in turn by another of the 1930 built Panniers numbered 7760 in 1961. Whilst the first went for scrap the second lasted until the end of steam on London Transport in 1971 and thus passed into preservation. ***Aldo Delicata***

Another one of the ex-Metropolitan Railway electric locomotives catches our eye next as 5 John Hampden takes an enthusiast's special along its old stomping ground near Neasden around 1960. ***Aldo Delicata***

The Metropolitan Railway F class was a design of 0-6-2T side tank steam locomotive. They were based on the earlier E Class. Four locomotives, numbered 90 to 93 were built by Yorkshire Engine Company in 1901. They were later numbered L49 to L52 and were based here at Neasden where the last was scrapped in 1962. ***Aldo Delicata***

Page right: Another one time regular at Neasden was this Peckett, which was acquired by the Metropolitan Railway in 1899 as No.101 in their fleet and went on to join London Transport as L53 and was withdrawn in 1960. ***Aldo Delicata***

LONDON TRANSPORT
L.53

Additional services into Metroland, the Chilterns and beyond could be found at Marylebone where we find on 10 June 1966 the 14:38 semi-fast for Nottingham, with Black Five 44920 providing the power. Steam services from here would cease just three months later and the line north from Aylesbury would be closed. ***Bill Wright***

Happier times on 18 April 1964, as 4472 Flying Scotsman has brought a railtour from Manchester Central via the Woodhead Tunnel to Marylebone and was being prepared for the return run when photographed alongside an English Electric Type 3. ***Strathwood Library Collection***

An exhibition of locomotives and rolling stock was held to celebrate the 50th Anniversary of the Institute of Locomotive Engineers, between 11 and 14 May 1961. This was the scene in the goods yard at Marylebone with a wide selection of steam, diesel and electric locomotives on display. Among the exhibits was the ex-Midland Railway 7'0" 3-cylinder Compound 4P 4-4-0 No. 1000, which was a Johnson locomotive of 1902, modified by Deeley in 1914. It was withdrawn in October 1951, but was selected for preservation and in June 1959 it was restored close to its 1914 condition with maroon livery. ***The Late Norman Browne/Strathwood Library Collection***

The former Great Western and Great Central joint lines run parallel with the Central Line at Northolt, where we see 70054 once named Dornoch Firth, heading for the capital on 7 October 1965 with a parcels service and nicely framed under a lower quadrant bracket giving the all clear for a down train. ***Aldo Delicata***

A return to the stretch between Neasden and Pinner to see 34002 Shaftesbury this time with a special on the RCTS organised Great Central Railtour on 13 August 1966. The tour took in an interesting route from Waterloo to Sheffield Victoria via Nottingham Victoria. ***Aldo Delicata***

We have already seen a number of photographs taken on the 4 March 1961 which our intrepid cameramen recorded together on a trip out to Watford and back from their homes in South London. This shot was taken at Moor Park with 10 William Ewart Gladstone heading an Aylesbury to Liverpool Street service which it has taken over at Rickmansworth. ***Frank Hornby***

Follow the Thames

Starting from the Chilterns we see the connecting service to Princes Risborough from here at Aylesbury in 1960 which was still in the hands of steam with 6421 running with the named autocoach Wren. ***Strathwood Library Collection***

Another Chiltern's route to Princes Risborough was from Oxford with several through trains to Paddington back along the joint lines, such as here at Thame with Modified Hall 6994 Baggrave Hall in 1960. ***Strathwood Library Collection***

Another Modified Hall 6963 Throwley Hall on 2 May 1965, reminds us that we can follow the route of the Thames into London from a southerly direction too, joining the mainline near Reading West from Basingstoke. ***Strathwood Library Collection***

Situated in the busy triangle of lines to the west of Reading General station was the shed coded 81D where we see 6815 Frilford Grange in 1964, the shed here closed to steam on 3 January 1965. ***Bob Treacher/Alton Model Centre***

A visit just before that closure was effected to 81D Reading rewards us with a fine line up in the winter sunshine with 6953 Leighton Hall among the other surviving Halls and 6100 Class Prairies. Reading's other shed was to the east of Reading General and Reading Southern stations, coded 70E it had closed to steam on 6 April 1964. ***Bob Treacher/Alton Model Centre***

Continueing our shed bash along the Thames we stop at Slough which is the junction for the branch to Windsor and Eton Central, the town was also served by the Southern Region with their branch from Staines. However it is a visit to 81B Slough that concerns us on 5 March 1961 where Prairie 6117 is among the Panniers that day. The use of Pressed Steel DMUs on local services was already making steam redundant at this time, the depot here closed completely on 1 June 1964. ***Frank Hornby***

One for lovers of steam as 6964 Thorley Hall helps a failed Hymek through Iver in August 1964, a not uncommon sight. ***Strathwood Library Collection***

As we head towards London we pass the Western Region's branches to Uxbridge Vine Street and Staines West that diverged from West Drayton, until we get to Southall for a trip down the branch to the docks on the Thames at Brentford. On 25 July 1965 with steam in full decline, the L.C.G.B. and the Railway Enthusiasts Club organised their Thames Valley Rail Tour using 6106, 46509, 80154 and 9773 seen here for the trips along the Western Region branches. ***Strathwood Library Collection***

Although 81C Southall was used to stable and service DMUs along the Thames Valley it was a modern structure improved in the previous decade for steam use and it still retained a lively selection of locomotives for a wide range of freight turns, some of which will no doubt employ 4700 and 4976 Warfield Hall in 1961. ***Strathwood Library Collection***

Taken the same day was another view with Prairie tank 6165 to the fore, the area around Southall was to become popular during the 1960s with immigrants from the Indian subcontinent. It lies close to Heathrow Airport which is itself a very large employer, but back in this decade a large number of factories could still be found within a few miles of Southall, all were hungry for employees at the time. ***Strathwood Library Collection***

DMUs have already evicted steam from the local services out of Paddington by 1 August 1964 leaving work for freight and standby use for failing diesels on passenger turns at Southall where we see 3820 in its last twelve months of service. ***Peter Coton***

Southall shed was used as stageing ground for redundant steam locomotives on their way to the scrap dealers of South Wales during the mid sixties, with many strangers laying over on their melancholy last journey. Although it is locally based Pannier 9659 that has caught our cameraman's attention on 22 May 1965, with the chalk markings reminding us of that promotion campaign run by ESSO at the time, with many a schoolboy wanting one of the fake tiger's tails to adorn their pushbike. ***Strathwood Library Collection***

The long footbridge crossing all the running lines, the Brentford branch and the entrance to the shed at Southall was always going to be a popular spot for spotters, your author included. Having pushed my luck on many an occasion by being late home for tea as a result of hanging on for just one more train, sound familiar? On 13 April 1963, 5988 Bostock Hall was making its way leisurely along the down slow with a return empty milk working. ***Frank Hornby***

Too soon for thoughts of preservation perhaps, but Class 9F 92203 appears to be in use for enthusiast's rides in the shed yard at 81C Southall on 13 November 1965. It would pass nearby along with 75029 on their way to preservation at the Longmoor Military Railway by the artist David Shepherd a few years later in what was thought at the time to be the last mainline steam to work through London. ***Strathwood Library Collection***

An easterley breeze is picking up the smoke from 6876 Kingsland Grange whilst stabled at Southall on 22 May 1965. Three days beforehand West Ham United became only the second British club to win a European trophy, defeating West German 1860 Munich 2-0 at Wembley Stadium. ***Peter Coton***

The distinctive and unique desert sand paint scheme given to D1000 Western Enterprise when released to traffic just before Christmas 1961 certainly made it stand out from the crowd and an easy spot as passes West Ealing on 28 June the following year, already showing exhaust markings on the paintwork. ***Dave Cobbe Collection/Rail Photoprints***

It seems everyone is looking out on the side of the train to catch what's on shed as they pass Old Oak Common on 11 June 1965. The significence of the numbers of enthusiasts onboard is that it is the last 16:15 Paddington to Banbury to be hauled by steam, in this case 7029 Clun Castle. ***Aldo Delicata***

We are beside another Castle Class in this view at Old Oak Common with 7036 Taunton Castle in July 1963. ***Win Wall/Strathwood Library Collection***

The warm early summer on 12 June 1963 has tempted at least two railway workers to enjoy the sunshine outside their bothy by the Old Oak Common coaling stage, whilst 7018 Drysllwyn Castle moves off with a full tender. ***Strathwood Library Collection***

One of the condensing variety of 5700 Class pannier tanks 9700 rests alongside the same coaling facility in 1962. This example was the only one of the eleven locomotives fitted with this apparatus not to have been built at Swindon Works. Instead this prototype was built by Beyer Peacock over two years before its classmates in 1931. ***Strathwood Library Collection***

Working our way around Old Oak Common we head next inside one of the large roundhouses to see what's on offer in July 1963. Identifiable today we have 1024 County of Pembroke, 3754, 9706, 6142 and a Castle all simmering nicely in shafts of sunlight. ***Win Wall/Strathwood Library Collection***

Back outside into the sunshine on New Year's Day 1961 to enjoy a reasonably well turned out 7024 Powis Castle moving light engine around the depot. Also on this day the farthing coin, used since the 13th century, ceased to be legal tender throughout the United Kingdom. ***Frank Hornby***

Keeping company with a Hawksworth pannier in 1963 was 9642, it was withdrawn from here the following year and consigned to the R.S.Hayes scrapyard at Bridgend. However, rather than being cut up it was used to shunt less fortunate locomotives that arrived for scrapping. Purchased in 1968 by the South Wales Pannier Group it moved to Maesteg Colliery where it worked coal traffic from time to time in its early days of preservation. ***Strathwood Library Collection***

7029

Afraid the end is nigh for 4701 and 7013 Bristol Castle at Old Oak Common on 29 May 1964. ***Peter Coton***

Page left: There is still plenty of active steam about when this view of 7029 Clun Castle was recorded in 1963. ***Strathwood Library Collection***

The site of the roundhouses at Old Oak Common gave way to open ground and the remaining famous turntable hosted diesels such as D845 Sprightly in April 1969, and D1695 in August 1966. ***Grahame Wareham & Frank Hornby***

Another fine view looking east towards the depot from the approach road to Old Oak Common on 14 August 1966, greets the spotter today with braces of Brush Type 4s, Hymeks and Westerns. In the news papers at the time we were disturbed by the Kray Twins who were being questioned in connection with a murder in London. Meanwhile in an unconnected crime three policemen were shot dead in London, whilst sitting in their patrol car in Shepherd's Bush, within a few days two suspects were arrested and charged with their murders.
Frank Hornby

Running light underneath Mitre Bridge on the approaches to Old Oak Common's extensive sidings was a real stranger on 23 October 1965 when Class A4 60007 Sir Nigel Gresley was chosen to work the A4 Preservation Society's Paddington Streamliner Rail Tour from Manchester Exchange to Paddington via Birmingham Snow Hill, the engine ran light for servicing to Southall. ***Strathwood Library Collection***

At Ranelagh Bridge the signal box still stands opposite London Transport's Royal Oak station in 1964 as D1000 Western Enterprise now blessed with yellow warning panels keeps company with a maroon classmate. ***Strathwood Library Collection***

Two rarities to Paddington but not to the capital were U Class 31639 and Q1 Class 33006 on 7 March 1965 with the Six Counties Rail Tour. Formed in 1955, and originally known as the Middlesex Loco Spotters Club, their name was changed in the late 1950's to the Home Counties Railway Club then in January 1963 it changed again, to the Home Counties Railway Society. This was the society's thirteenth railtour, and very last tour unfortunately. ***Winston Cole***

Two shots from the same platform location at Paddington just a couple of summers apart demonstrate the air of change on the Western Region in it's fury to be the first region to be steam free, firstly with 5011 Tintagel Castle in 1962. ***Richard Icke***

Secondly the crew of Hymek D7029 await their release light engine back to Ranelagh Bridge stabling point, after the stock they arrived with has left in July 1964. By the end of the decade the writing was on the wall for the era of hydraulic traction as well. ***Noel Marrison***

The great expanse of crossovers on the approaches to Paddington would be rationalised after steam ended at the station, but for now on 31 August 1963, Prairie Tank 6135 wears pilot number 14 as it shuffles around this busy terminus. Musically at this time we would see Billy J. Kramer and the Dakotas lose their top spot in the charts to The Beatles with She Loves You. ***Peter Coton***

It was a cold and rainy day for the running of the LCGB's Paddington Steam Farewell Rail Tour on 20 November 1965 which saw 4079 Pendennis Castle run throughout to Worcester, Cheltenham, Gloucester and back via Swindon. ***Aldo Delicata***

A week later and its another rainy day for the departure of 7029 Clun Castle from Paddington on 27 November 1965, for the official British Rail Farewell to Steam. Gabardine macs are much in evidence among the cameramen present on the day. The special worked out via Swindon to Bristol and Gloucester where the weather was much kinder to photographers, although D1006 Western Stalwart worked the train from Gloucester to Cheltenham and back, handing over to 7029 Clun Castle once more for a run to Swindon where D6881 and D6882 were waiting as the motive power for the return to Paddington. ***Strathwood Library Collection***

South Western Approach

Still carrying her nameplates was Standard 5MT 73116 Iseult in May 1964 with a service ready to depart from London's Waterloo station under the overall roof. ***Late Norman Browne/Strathwood Library Collection***

The headcode suggests the blue 4-TC set alongside 34052 Lord Dowding is bound for Southampton as the line beyond Basingstoke was now electrified almost to Bournemouth from Waterloo. ***Michael Beaton***

A few years before and another busy scene at Waterloo with a rebuilt Bulleid Pacific, this time 34014 Budleigh Salterton draws in whilst Standard Class 3MT's 82023 and 82027 attend as pilots on 3 October 1964. ***Strathwood Library Collection***

It was to be a well polished pair of U Class locomotives led by 31791 with 31639 that would take out the RCTS organised Longmoor Rail Tour from Waterloo on 30 April 1966. ***Aldo Delicata***

Whereas the condition of 34025 Whimple leaves much to be desired as its hard to recognise any signs of lined green livery when seen in May 1965 at Waterloo. ***The Late Norman Brown/Strathwood Library Collection***

Happily the prospect of railtour duty has brought 35028 Clan Line to the attention of the cleaners as it prepares to depart Waterloo on Sunday 27 February 1966 with the Dorset Belle Rail Tour sponsored by the LCGB. ***Peter Coton***

A fine rake of Southern Region green coaches trails behind M7 Class 30049, as it works hard up the bank from Waterloo and past Vauxhall with ecs for Clapham Junction on 16 September 1961, no doubt pressed with the need to clear the sections as quickly as the crew can ahead of electric services on the Windsor Lines. ***Frank Hornby***

A young lad looks out onto the wilderness that has befallen 70A Nine Elms in early July 1967, the depot would close completely on the 9th of the month as steam ended on the Southern Region. The last few stragglers of withdrawn steam locomotives would be dragged away heading for South Wales via Salisbury as the next few weeks passed. ***The Late Ken Pullen/Strathwood Library Collection***

A visit to London in the summer of 1964 for one cameraman from the North East prompted this view of 35004 Cunard White Star, this would be one of the earlier withdrawls among the Merchant Navy Pacifics meaning it would be cut up fifteen months before the end of Southern Region steam operations. ***Noel Marrison***

Better fortune would befall Class E4 32473 still in service as a yard pilot during 1962 at Nine Elms, as it would be purchased for preservation and make its way to the still fledgling Bluebell Railway once withdrawn that November. ***Strathwood Library Collection***

A pair of Merchant Navy Pacifics were being made ready to depart from Nine Elms to take up service, led by 35025 Brocklebank Line on 29 May 1964. Although the photographer would not know it at the time, this example would be another of her class to be withdrawn a few months later to be sent join the swelling ranks at Barry in South Wales. ***Peter Coton***

A view not so frequently recorded at Nine Elms was looking back to the exit roads seen here with 34034 Honiton making the most of the squalor towards the end of steam as it takes water on 29 April 1967. ***David Rostance/Rail Photoprints***

Much of this dishevelled appearance around the shed at Nine Elms on 25 February 1961 can be attributed to the actions of the Luftwaffe, as it was a favourite target for them during the blitz. However it will not be long before North British built Class L1 31783 will be made redundant. Fifteen of her class joined British Railways in 1948, but only one will survive to see service by the end of this year. ***Frank Hornby***

A degree of apparent respectability adorns 35022 Holland America Line outside in the sunshine and among the ever present ash around Nine Elms on 6 March 1965. ***Dave Cobbe/Rail Photoprints***

Southern Suburbs

We have taken a Southern Electric service out to Feltham in February 1963 in search of the last two withdrawn Urie Class G16's. One of these was 30494 which was stabled with other withdrawn locomotives such as 30346 and 31923 in a long line behind the cemetery. ***Strathwood Library Collection***

Another visit to 70B Feltham the year beforehand on 28 January threw up Class E6 32416, looking down and out and about to be officially withdrawn. ***Strathwood Library Collection***

As with all depots with a steam allocation the fitters would have to make many locomotives fit to travel sometimes long distances without any working lubrication, after months and sometimes years out of use. Taken out of service in January 1964 was Maunsell Class S15 30841, it was stripped of any restrictions that might run hot for its journey to Woodham's scrapyard at Barry and breaking up. It would of course be one of the lucky survivors, whereas many would be less fortunate, such as Standard 4MT 80133 seen the same day, although it managed to live on until July 1967 in service. ***Both: Strathwood Library Collection***

Preservation and a return to their glory years and pre-grouping liveries for Drummond Class T9 120 and Caledonian Railway 123 in steam for a special on shed at Norwood Junction on 15 September 1963. Coded 75C, Norwood Junction shed was built by the Southern Railway in 1935 and closed to steam on 6 January 1964 and completely on 21 August 1966. ***Strathwood Library Collection***

Another Southern Railway built shed was at Hither Green coded 73C, being on the Eastern Section it closed to steam in October 1961 as part of the effects of the Kent Coast electrification. On 4 February 1967 it was host to BRC&W Type 3s and Electro-Diesels and a Drewry Class 04. ***Colin Rodgers/Strathwood Library Collection***

Also serving the Kent Coast and the former South Eastern & Chatham Railway's routes was 73B Bricklayers Arms shed which closed completely on 18 June 1962. Looking smart on shed the year beforehand, was Schools Class 30931 King's Wimbledon, which was scrapped that October within a month of being posted as withdrawn. ***Strathwood Library Collection***

The same smart scrapping process at Ashford Works would befall Class E1 31507, seen here simmering too outside Bricklayers Arms in the sunshine on 24 April 1961, it was withdrawn in July and cut up completely the following month. ***Strathwood Library Collection***

A search for clean mainline express locomotives brings us to 73A Stewarts Lane on 6 June 1962 for Schools Class 30926 Repton, looking in fine fettle and prepared for the Royal Train to attend that year's Derby at Epsom, in which there was uproar as there were seven horses who fell in a race without any fences! ***Dave Cobbe/Rail Photoprints***

Just before the service went over to electric locomotives we see 34100 Appledore turned out with the full Golden Arrow regalia on 8 June 1961 at Stewarts Lane. ***Dave Cobbe/Rail Photoprints***

The mighty structure of Battersea Power Station stands sentinel over Schools Class 30901 Winchester, which was prepared as the standby locomotive for the Royal Train at Stewarts Lane on 8 June 1962 for the Derby Day race meeting and a special to Tattenham Corner station. ***Dave Cobbe/Rail Photoprints***

A pairing of Class L1, 31786 and Class D1, 31749 make ready for the off from Victoria on 11 June 1961 with the LCGB's running of the South Eastern Limited Rail Tour. This was an extremely well filled tour, it was originally planned to have a load of seven Hastings line restriction 0 corridor vehicles. When applications flooded in the LCGB requested more vehicles, but as the line had gone over to DEMU operation it seems that there was no more corridor stock of the right loading gauge available. To accommodate all those wishing to participate two ex SE&CR non-corridor coaches, known as S 100's were added to the formation. In a letter sent out with the tickets, passengers with tickets numbered over 250 were requested to use the non-corridor stock which, it was estimated, would be filled only with eight passengers per compartment instead of the twelve seating capacity. Because of the increased load the train was double headed throughout, except on the Kent & East Sussex section where only seven vehicles were used, and the train was top & tailed. Due to the response received all passengers received a refund of 2/- per head, which was handed out when tickets were inspected. ***Strathwood Library Collection***

Below: Just a few minutes before departure from Victoria in 1960 for Battle of Britain 34085 501 Squadron with another service for the Kent Coast. ***Robin Brown Collection***

Page right: One of those then new Hastings DEMUs has just arrived at Cannon Street in 1960 and has just begun disgorging its passengers under what was left of the overall roof. The station, which had been subject to structural neglect prior to the Second World War, suffered extensive bomb damage during the blitz and was hit by several incendiary devices which damaged the roof. A high explosive also hit no. 8 platform. The original glass roof had been removed before the war in an attempt to save it, ironically the factory in which the roof was stored was itself badly bombed, destroying the roof. ***Strathwood Library Collection***

1003

Majestic Midland

Ready for departure to Manchester Central at St.Pancras in the summer of 1965 was one of the two six car Midland Pullman sets looking out from underneath the impressive William Barlow designed train shed, which in 1868 when it opened, was the largest single-span roof in the world. ***Noel Marrison***

Looking back along the Euston Road to the front of St. Pancras station on 27 May 1961, it is hard to consider the planners thought at the time that the redevelopement of Euston station would make this award winning station and hotel designed by George Gilbert Scott redundant and suitable for demolition. Several attempts were made to close it and demolish the hotel, these attempts provoked strong and successful opposition, with the campaign led by the later Poet Laureate, John Betjeman. ***Frank Hornby***

Fairburn designed 4MT 42156 was based upon the earlier Stanier 2-6-4T with a shorter wheelbase and weighing two tons less. Built at Derby Works in 1948 it was part of a post war programme of modernisation that saw it cast aside for scrap early in 1966. However in 1960 it was still finding work on ecs underneath the twenty four arches constructed by The Butterley Company based firmly in Midland Railway territory at Ripley in Derbyshire. ***Winston Cole***

Another display of fine Victorian ironwork is seen with the gas holders in the background to a brand new BRC&W Type 2 D5404 just delivered on 4 August 1962 and engaged also on ecs duties at St. Pancras. ***Peter Coton***

Services in and out from the Midland Railway's London terminus and extensive goods yards were supplied by engines from 14A Cricklewood and here at 14B Kentish Town. Where on a visit in June 1960 we find Standard 5MT 73014 about to be made obsolete with fresh deliveries of Peak diesels. ***Ian Turnbull/Rail Photoprints***

Keeping company around the open roundhouse with Royal Scot 46139 The Welch Regiment was named Class B1 61034 Chiru which is named after a Tibetan species of antelope. The shed here at Kentish Town would close completely in April 1963, with Cricklewood picking up the work from then onwards. ***Ian Turnbull/Rail Photoprints***

A pleasant surprise perhaps on 3 March 1963 at Cricklewood to find Class V2 60876 taking coal, but then maybe not since the closure of 14D Neasden on 18 June 1962 which had been responsible for servcing locomotives off the former Great Central route into Marylebone. ***Strathwood Library Collection***

92156

In the early 1960s it was still commonplace for a vast amount of coal to be delivered daily to London to supply the capital's need for domestic heating and power generation. Shunting some empties for their return to the coalfields of Derbyshire and Nottinghamshire at Brent South sidings on 1 September 1964, was Jinty tank 47432. Also engaged in the yard that day was Austerity 2-8-0 90388. ***Both: Strathwood Library Collection***

Page left: A terrible waste of resources best describes Class 9F 92156, with not much left of a working life of just under ten years when it was seen stabled among the diesels at Cricklewood on 17 August 1963. ***Frank Hornby***

Kings Cross Modernisation

Whilst consideration for closure was being made about the Midland neighbours next door at St. Pancras, much had been spent in the previous decade on improvements to the southern stretches of the East Coast Main Line, with quadrupling of the track and rebuilding some very tired suburban stations. As a result Kings Cross's future looked certain, although a comparison with both stations with how they are today will open a few eyes. At the start of the decade the modern world still looked like this with two Baby Deltics adding their fumes to the gloomy atmosphere. At the same time Prime Minister Harold Macmillan makes the 'Wind of Change' speech. In the London 60,000 protestors staged a demonstration against nuclear weapons, and Burnley went on to win the Division One title. The Shadows' instrumental Apache was released, oh and a four-strong male band from Liverpool, performed their first concert under the name of The Beatles in Hamburg, in West Germany. ***Robin Brown Collection***

Page right: The old order carried on for a few more years at least, with 60006 Sir Ralph Wedgewood now weeks away from steam's dismissal from the Cross on 17 February 1963, and 60015 Quicksilver likewise heading north again on 7 July 1962. ***Douglas Twibble & Frank Hornby***

60006

M2
60015

More serious servicing for steam locomotives would be carried out at 34A Kings Cross affectionately known as Top Shed, we find Class A3 60063 Isinglass present on 3 March 1963 and 60022 Mallard two years beforehand. It would close completely on 15 June 1963 with the end of regular steam operations, leaving just the servicing facility at the station for diesels. ***Photos: Strathwood Library Collection & Frank Hornby***

Throughout the decade the traditional style of railway operation could still be enjoyed by the spotters at the platform ends at Kings Cross, albeit with diesel locomotives and the to and fro they required to clear the station throat and gain access to the stabling point. In June 1966 we can see two of the main players for the next twenty years until full electrification rendered both Brush designs surplus here and the closure in turn of the stabling point. ***Grahame Wareham***

Fitting substitutes for Gresley, Thompson and Peppercorn Pacifics in the eyes of diesel enthusiasts at least but not in the eyes of die hard steam men were the

twenty two Deltics. To service the new fleet of diesel classes a new depot facility was built at Finsbury Park, and coded 34G when it opened on 24 April 1960. As duties were turned over to the new traction it allowed nearby Hornsey 34B to be closed to steam on 11 June 1961, with final closure coming in 1971. Alongside the new depot at Finsbury Park in June 1966 was D9000 Royal Scots Grey, whilst inside the shed in 1964 was an ex-works D5662 in the company of two more Brush products. ***Photos: Grahame Wareham & Noel Marrison***

D5673
D5662
D 1547

Great Eastern Rennaisance

It seems most enthusiasts with a camera who visited Liverpool Street at the start of the 1960s were taken to photograph Class J69 68619, which had been specially repainted into a mock version of the former Great Eastern Railway's lined blue livery to act as one of the station pilots. Just as well really as this popular locomotive was withdrawn in October 1961 and scrapped the same month at Stratford Works. ***Strathwood Libary Collection***

Although more popular with cameramen than other City of London termini such as Broad Street, Fenchurch Street, Holborn Viaduct, Blackfriars and London Bridge the oppressive dark nature of Liverpool Street through the 1960s, certainly made it difficult to achieve satisfactory results with very slow speed colour film. Although fortunately some did give it a go, such as here on the concourse in 1962 and out in the sunshine with a Clacton train ready to depart on 25 July 1966. ***Photos: Strathwood Library Collection & Peter Simmonds***

Replacements for the Britannias, B17 Footballers and Thompson B1s would arrive in the shape of English Electric Type 4's and Type 3's with a supporting cast of Brush Type 2's. Although the likes of D204 and her classmates on the Great Eastern section would be moved north soon after this 1964 view was taken. ***Douglas Twibble***

On 6 October 1962 D8236 was rostered to head a five coach RCTS organised tour from Liverpool Street of East London's goods lines and closed passenger routes as far as it could run along them, this included the Silvertown Tramway, where it set off at 13:36 managing to cover 88 miles by its return at 18:51. ***Douglas Twibble***

The period from 1958 to 1961 decimated the one hundred and thirty-four Class N7's under a surge of EMU and DMU deliveries, line closures, and new diesel locomotives. The last nine soldiered on into 1962, one of those withdrawn at Christmas 1960, was 69701 seen here on a down local near Bethnal Green on 11 July the same year. ***Douglas Twibble***

Perhaps more fortunate to last a while longer was 69714 parked up at Stratford next to a Metropolitan Cammell DMU in October 1961, it had been withdrawn however two weeks beforehand and would be cut up by the end of the month in the works here. ***The Late Norman Browne/ Strathwood Library Collection***

Fully prepared for another shift with a charge of coal was Class Y4 numbered 33 in the Departmental series for work around Stratford on 27 February 1960. ***Alan Pike OBE***

Stabled in the rows alongside Stratford's distinctive ferro-concrete coaler on 7 October 1961 was Class J15, 65462 which would evade the efficient cutting processes of Stratford Works when withdrawn the following September and be kept for preservation instead. ***The Late Vincent Heckford/Strathwood Library Collection***

The cutting staff still had to be kept busy and these three including Class J20 64697 in the rows at Stratford in October 1961 will not last too long as the Hill designed 0-6-0 will have gone during following month. ***The Late Norman Browne/Strathwood Library Collection***

Better luck would befall Holden's Class B12, 61572 also recorded the same day at Stratford as it fell into the arms of preservationists, whilst the first of its type had been withdrawn in 1948 without even recieving it's allocated British Railway's number of 61500. ***The Late Norman Browne/Strathwood Library Collection***

A posed official publicity view on behalf of English Electric inside one Stratford's running sheds in the mid sixties, makes the most of their Type 4, 3 and 1 designs, no doubt after asking for the removal of any Brush Type 4 and 2 designs beforehand. ***Strathwood Library Collection***

Attempts to keep some of the very littly laden routes open led to the trials of several railbus designs, including this one seen at Stratford on 7 October 1961, numbered E79964 from Waggon und Machinbau which came to British Railways in April 1958. The five examples of this type were deemed uncomfortable and un-reliable and offered for resale or scrap in 1966. Four of the five including this machine were purchased by preservation concerns. ***Late Vincent Heckford/Strathwood Library Collection***

Opposite: We close with a view of Class J15, 65476 surrounded by the paraphernalia of the modern railway as it was at Chingford, on 7 April 1962 at the head of the Great Eastern Suburban Rail Tour. ***Late Vincent Heckford/Strathwood Library Collection***

LCGB
THE GREAT EASTERN
SUBURBAN RAIL TOUR
65476

Help To Preserve Our Railway Heritage

Strathwood not only publish books on our railway heritage but have also set up the Railway Photographic Preservation Association as a Charitable Trust to house an archive of images comprising over 200,000 photographic negatives and slides.

The archive was established to not only preserve the collections of over one hundred photographers both living and deceased, but to also make their work available to a younger audience for the future. To achieve this aim, we have begun an energetic programme to publish a considerable number of books. Allied to this we are making as many as possible of the photographs and slides we hold, available as copies to interested enthusiasts, individuals, societies and other publishers.

Many photographers have chosen Strathwood to care for their collections and to publish the best examples of their work for posterity.

If you have negatives or colour slides of transport subjects then we would like to hear from you. We purchase, accept on loan, or welcome donations of material to the archive. Photographers always receive recognition for their work when it is used by publishers (A N Other/Strathwood Library). To answer why so many images are just credited as Strathwood Library Collection in this volume, the reason is we do not know who the original photographer was. This is usually because their collection gets split up via auctions or collectors upon their death with no record of the late photographer for us to credit. Please do not let this happen to your collection. Make contact with us today to discuss what can be done to ensure you work is fully credited and recognised for both today and the future.

Please call us today if you would like to see your work in print, perhaps in a similar fashion to this publication. We also undertake publications to benefit charities and societies on behalf of our contributors. In addition we can store, and catalogue collections on behalf of clubs and societies by way of loan, thereby releasing such groups to concentrate on other aspects of their activities.

Strathwood,
9 Boswell Crescent,
Inverness, IV2 3ET.

Telephone 01463 234004

www.strathwood.co.uk

Don't leave it any longer! YOU can then see YOUR work in print.